'Insightful, helpful, encouraging, hopeful and compassionate from beginning to end! The authors skillfully embed PDA strategies throughout the book to allow the child a sense of autonomy and control throughout that will, hopefully, be a rewarding and cathartic experience for all. I sincerely wish that this book had been available when my daughter and I first began navigating this most complex of journeys and I can't recommend it highly enough to those who are now beginning, or struggling in, theirs.'

– *Jane Sherwin, author of* Pathological Demand Avoidance
Syndrome – My Daughter is not Naughty

'I think that one of the best ways to help your PDA child is to support them to gain insight in a nonjudgmental and open way. Helping them communicate this to you helps them feel understood and then empowers you as their advocate. It also helps you as the parent see all those truly wonderful positives about your PDA child. This book provides a wonderful framework for doing that.'

– *Cassandra Davies, parent of a young person with PDA and
member of PDA Action Group Somerset and PDA, Pathological
Demand Avoidance Support – Families & Practitioners UK*

'Glòria and Tamar's book is an essential read for children and young people with PDA and their families. Me and My PDA is packed with pages which encourage young people with PDA to develop their understanding of Pathological Demand Avoidance, and create their own supportive strategies.'

– *Sarah Wild, Headteacher of Limpsfield Grange*

'Thank you, Tamar and Glòria, for helping me give my children and many more to come the chance to have their voice heard.'

– *parent of a child with PDA*

'This book provides a helpful, informative and personalised framework to help young people make sense of their PDA profile with support from their families and other adults they know. Its strengths are in its flexibility, in its regard for promoting emotional wellbeing and in the key messages it highlights about individuality and the importance of devising strategies collaboratively.'

– *Ruth Fidler, education consultant in complex autism, author of* Can I
tell you about Pathological Demand Avoidance syndrome?

by the same authors

My Autism Book

A Child's Guide to their Autism Spectrum Diagnosis

Glòria Durà-Vilà and Tamar Levi

ISBN 978 1 84905 438 6

eISBN 978 0 85700 868 8

of related interest

Can I tell you about Pathological Demand Avoidance syndrome?

A guide for friends, family and professionals

Ruth Fidler and Phil Christie

Illustrated by Jonathon Powell

ISBN 978 1 84905 513 0

eISBN 978 0 85700 929 6

Part of the *Can I tell you about...?* series

Pathological Demand Avoidance Syndrome – My Daughter is Not Naughty

Jane Alison Sherwin

ISBN 978 1 84905 614 4

eISBN 978 1 78450 085 6

Understanding Pathological Demand Avoidance Syndrome in Children

A Guide for Parents, Teachers and Other Professionals

Phil Christie, Margaret Duncan, Ruth Fidler and Zara Healy

ISBN 978 1 84905 074 6

eISBN 978 0 85700 253 2

Part of the *JKP Essentials* series

Collaborative Approaches to Learning for Pupils with PDA

Strategies for Education Professionals

Ruth Fidler and Phil Christie

ISBN 978 1 78592 017 2

eISBN 978 1 78450 261 4

ME AND MY PDA

A Guide to Pathological Demand Avoidance
for Young People

Glòria Durà-Vilà and Tamar Levi

Jessica Kingsley *Publishers*
London and Philadelphia

First published in 2019
by Jessica Kingsley Publishers
73 Collier Street
London N1 9BE, UK
and
400 Market Street, Suite 400
Philadelphia, PA 19106, USA

www.jkp.com

Copyright © Glòria Durà-Vilà and Tamar Levi 2019
Cover art and content illustration source: Tamar Levi.

Library of Congress Cataloging in Publication Data
A CIP catalog record for this book is available from the Library of Congress

British Library Cataloguing in Publication Data
A CIP catalogue record for this book is available from the British Library

ISBN 978 1 78592 465 1
eISBN 978 1 78450 849 4

Printed and bound in China

To David and our amazing children, Josep and Mireia. (Glòria)

With love and gratitude for the support of my mother Sarah, the professional opinions of my sister Dalia Levi, the constant motivation of my husband Vasilis Katsardis and the distracting entertainment of our daughter Tova Niovi. (Tamar)

Acknowledgements

The author team would like to acknowledge the children who were under Dr Glòria Durà-Vilà's care and who bravely let us into their world so we could understand it. We are also very grateful to their parents who were such strong advocates for their children and who worked with Glòria to offer the best possible care for them. You inspired and compelled us to write this book.

We cannot let this opportunity go by without paying tribute to a heroine of the publishing world, Jessica Kingsley, whom we are going to miss enormously after her retirement. Many thanks, Jessica, for your enthusiasm for our work and for your unique contribution to the literature on autism and mental health; it has been an honour and a privilege to publish our work with you.

This is a letter to you.
It could be called The Preface.
This means it's at the beginning of the book.

Dear YOU,

We have written this book **for you**. You are **in control** of this book **at all times**. You can read it whenever you like. It doesn't matter how long it takes you to go through the book, weeks or years, or if you choose to give some pages a miss – it doesn't matter at all! You can choose to read it by yourself or with someone else. It is also up to you to decide whom you want to share it with.

You are an **expert**. You know yourself better than anyone else. If anyone wanted to know anything about how you feel, what you think and how you see the world, **you are the best teacher there is**.

The goal of this book is that you **understand what PDA means for you**. This will help you and those adults close to you to develop your talents and to find ways to cope better with your difficulties.

We have put a lot of information about PDA in here. **No two people with these difficulties are the same**

so it would be great if you could help find which bits are right for you and which bits are not. We would love to learn how **your PDA is unique**. This is so you and the important people around you – your parents, teachers or other trusted grown-ups – can have a better understanding of how PDA affects you. You are the very best person to tell us about your PDA.

Wishing you all the best,

Glòria and *Tamar*

Two people wrote this book together. We will introduce ourselves now:

Hello, I'm Dr Glòria!

99.9 per cent of my patients call me Dr Glòria, which is easier to remember than my surname.

I studied medicine and child and adolescent psychiatry, and I specialise in Autism Spectrum Disorder.

Let me tell you how the book came to be: over the years, many children and young people who were told they had PDA have asked me to help them understand what having PDA was all about, and even more importantly, what PDA meant specifically for them. Many parents and teachers have also asked how best to help children and pupils to understand their difficulties. I thought it would be easier if I made a book that you could take home, to look at any time you wanted. Also, parents and people who help you can read it to understand and support you better.

As I did with my earlier child's guide to Autism Spectrum Disorder, *My Autism Book*, I asked Tamar to help me with the book. She didn't need much convincing this time either as she loved the idea straightaway. I will let Tamar introduce herself now.

Hi, I'm Tamar!

It's my job to explain things. Sometimes I explain things in pictures, as an artist for books. Sometimes I explain things as an author by writing them down. Sometimes I explain things in the classroom as a teacher. I spend all my time explaining things!

Dr Glòria told me all she knows about PDA and we worked hard figuring out how to explain it together. Plus, I'm a member of social media groups where I check with parents, carers and families how they would like to explain PDA too.

I made sure we left space for you to write and draw too. If you notice something missing, you can also write your own words in this book or make your own pictures to explain your own PDA.

This is a letter for your parents. You can share it with them if you want to.

Dear Parents,

We witness again and again, with awe and admiration, how you have bravely undergone the journey to understand your child's difficulties and to get the best support for them. Some of you found that descriptions of PDA 'made perfect sense', that it described difficulties you were having while trying your best to parent your child. Many talked about a 'penny dropping' moment when reading about PDA. We listened and heard that your paths have been plagued with misunderstanding, confusion, controversy, ignorance, disbelief and even judgement coming from professionals. We were even told that some of you were refused help by services as PDA is not in the diagnostic classifications. Whatever name we might give to a child's difficulties, it must never reduce their complexity into a meaningless label; a diagnosis should never put children into a box. On the contrary, it should **help people understand their strengths and difficulties**. This book aims to support **a 'needs-led' individualised programme** full of strategies and approaches that is shared by you, your family and friends, and all the professionals involved in the care of your child.

It is the parents of young people with PDA, with their immense tenacity and determination to help their children, who fight most for recognition among education, mental health and social care services. They do all this whilst also forming worldwide societies and online forums to share useful information and to support each other.

The authors of this book have pooled skills from a range of professions: we come from mental health and education backgrounds, with expertise in communicating complicated ideas in simple language and pictures. Listening to young people with these difficulties and their parents inspired us to write this book. Parents and other professionals told us that our earlier publication, *My Autism Book: A Child's Guide to their Autism Spectrum Disorder*, was useful for the more 'classic' presentation of Autism Spectrum Disorder (ASD) but didn't capture PDA characteristics. Parents wanted a book written for children and young people with the difficulties associated with PDA, a book that their child could own, to be used as a platform to explore their very unique set of challenges and difficulties within ASD and the concrete ways to manage their difficulties that work for them. We also listened to young people asking questions about the differences that they had noted when comparing themselves to others their age and felt that they didn't 'fit in with their peers'. Answering these questions in a way that makes sense to the young person can indeed be difficult. Our book wants to support the process of gradually creating self-awareness in the young person as it gently invites them to address these complicated but key questions in a clear and sensitive manner. It also aims to develop, in collaboration with your child, a repertoire of tailor-made problem-solving strategies and to provide a shared language that can be used by you and your child to communicate about PDA.

Although this process is a long one and very likely to be filled with plenty of bumps, the goal is clear: for your child to gain a better understanding of themselves, of their talents and limitations, as they mature into adulthood. In our experience, the benefits of this process will compensate for the challenges by a huge margin. Nothing could be more worthwhile!

Making better sense of themselves can help your child to improve their self-esteem as they realise that they are not alone in their struggles; they become aware of strengths that can then be fostered leading them to forge a more positive conception of themselves. It will also guide the search for better ways to manage their difficulties and problematic behaviours. In the long term, it will help them to make the right choices for the future. When you, or other trusted people involved in your child's life, think they are ready for these conversations, we hope this book could be a good starting point, and a way to keep these important conversations going.

With every good wish on your journey,

Glòria and *Tamar*

What does PDA mean?

You may have noticed that there are some differences between you and others. You might feel, especially on those days when nothing goes your way, that you struggle with things that others seem to be able to do more easily. You may wonder why other kids around you seem to just get on with other people and other things.

A psychologist named **Elizabeth Newson** gave a name to describe the particular set of strengths and difficulties that young people like you have in common: Pathological Demand Avoidance, or **PDA** for short. Nowadays PDA is also referred to as Extreme Demand Avoidance.

We could explain it by saying that your brain is wired in a different way from that of most people. However, there are lots of other people whose brain is wired in a similar way to yours. It is not useful to compare people's brains as everyone's brain is unique. Your brain is not better or worse than any other's.

Why bother with this book?

Our brain will be with us for life: we can't get a different brain from the one we were born with, so it's wise for all of us to learn how to make the most of our own brain. A good way to do this is to learn as much as possible about yourself. This is the aim of this book: to help you to **understand yourself better**. Understanding how PDA affects you is an important part of this process.

We have given our best to this book to help you with such an important and worthy task. We would like you to think of our book as a tool. A tool to help make better sense of yourself so you can find ways to help yourself to pursue your dreams and ultimately lead a **happy and wonderful life.**

In the next pages, the book invites you to do lots of things: to find out about your strengths and difficulties, to look for ways to foster your strengths and to develop strategies to manage your difficulties in a way that works for you. It would be great if you decide to share your findings with the most important people in your life so you can get the help and support you need. **It is very important that the grown-ups caring for you know how they can make things better for you.**

15

At the end of the book, there will be a few pages dedicated to summarising the difficulties you have identified and the strategies that you have found that are helpful. Your parents and those caring for you may want to photocopy these summary pages so everyone can access them easily and keep them in mind. There will also be space to tell us, if you wish to do so, about any other difficulties and strategies that have not been included here.

Autism Spectrum Disorder and PDA

Before PDA was described, many strengths and differences were grouped together under one name: Autism Spectrum Disorder, or ASD for short. You share the main characteristics of ASD as well as sharing the main characteristics of PDA. So you have a diagnosis of Autism Spectrum Disorder with these other features which can be called PDA.

What PDA is *not*

PDA is *not* your fault or your family's fault. It is not anyone's fault. Each person's brain is different: some people are better at some things than others are and some people find some things much more difficult than others do. People with PDA did not choose to find some things difficult.

PDA is *not* an illness. You must not worry about PDA making you physically unwell. It will not go away but it will not hurt you. It will become easier with time as you learn how to deal with the difficulties and make the most of your many strengths. It's good to remember that PDA certainly does not prevent you from having a wonderful and meaningful life!

Your PDA does *NOT* define you

On a very bad day you may feel that your PDA is the whole world, everything you can see and feel. You might think it is all that you are, and that there is nothing left of you. We can assure you that you are much MUCH more than your PDA.

PDA is part of who you are but not all!
You are not defined by your PDA. Although young people with PDA have similarities, PDA does not define someone because it is different for each person.

Each person with PDA is unique.
We have written this book to help you to find your description of PDA: what PDA means for **you**.

Important facts about YOU

It would be great to know some facts about you that have nothing to do with your PDA. You may want to start by writing down what you most enjoy doing.

- My hobbies are / I really like to:

. . . .

You may want to write the names of the most important people in your life.

- My favourite people are:

. . . .

You may have a pet that is very dear to you.

- My pet is a:

. . . .

and my pet's name is:

. . . .

Do you have a favourite toy or game that you prefer to the rest of your other toys or games?

• My favourite toy/game is:

....

How do you like to relax?

• I chill out by:

....

Let's explore what you are good at.

• I'm good at:

....

• You may want to ask your parents what makes them proud to be your parent and write it here:

....

If you want to, you can write or draw any facts about yourself here. You can also add any that we have not included in this book. You can change this at any time.

19

You may want to do a drawing of your hobbies, your favourite toy or a drawing of yourself doing something you are good at in the box below. You may want to write down any interesting things about yourself too.

Fancy using your wonderful **imagination**? How about doing a little **acting** or **role-playing**?

A teacher is someone who explains things. Could you become a teacher from now on? In your role as a teacher, you are faced with a very important question: **what does PDA mean for YOU?** We are all eager to learn the answer from you!

To help you to answer the question, we have written down the difficulties that children and young people with PDA have shared with us. We have also gathered some of the strategies that have helped them to cope better with their difficulties.

It is very important to clarify before you start that **not all of the difficulties and strategies mentioned here will be applicable to you**. As there are no two people with PDA who are the same, you may want to tick the difficulties and strategies that apply to you and add those that we have missed.

Also, some of the things you identify with today may well change in time as you grow and learn new ways to cope. The things you struggle with today may even change (become more or less troublesome) depending on the way you feel or what is going on around you. Therefore, it may be a good idea to use **pencil** so you can change things you've written and erase things that are no longer difficult for you.

So, are you up for doing a little acting as our teacher? I bet you can teach us all what you are finding out about your PDA as you go through the book. In your role as our teacher you can tell us which of the struggles people with PDA may have apply to you, and which ways of dealing with their difficulties work for you.

We would like you to remember that:

You are the best teacher about YOU.
You are the expert about YOU.
Your parents, teachers and everyone who cares for you
and is part of your life are really looking forward to
learning from YOU about YOU.

You may want to do a drawing of yourself here dressed up as a **teacher**. In your picture, you may be teaching a lot of people, or just the most important people in your life. Would you prefer to be sitting down or standing up, walking around while explaining or writing it all down? If you prefer to dress yourself up as one, you could ask your mother, father or a teacher to take a picture of you in your very own teacher costume and stick it up here, or you may prefer to take a selfie.

So, teacher, are you ready to prepare a whole lesson about your PDA? Shall we get our pencils out and start reading and ticking boxes?

Or maybe you prefer someone else to read it out loud and tick the boxes for you? Your choice!

Challenges You May Struggle With

Demands, demands and more demands!

We have learned from the children and young people with PDA we have met that they struggle a lot to cooperate with demands.

We have learned from them how incredibly anxious being asked to do things can sometimes make them feel.

You may find it very hard to do what others want you to do

☐ Do you feel that the world is forcing you to behave in certain ways that you don't want to, that you don't see the point of?

☐ Do you feel people around you are placing constant demands on you that you are unable to meet?

☐ Do you find it very hard to do what your parents and teachers ask you to do, even things you know you are able to do?

- [ ] Do you think you have the same rights as the adults around you – such as your parents and teachers – and don't understand why you should do what they tell you to do?

- [ ] Some young people with PDA have told us that they struggle when their parents ask them to do the things they need to do to get ready in the morning or to go to bed, such as getting dressed or brushing their teeth. Do you find these routines difficult?

- [ ] Do you find it hard to do something if it is asked using a sign, for example, 'Don't walk on the grass' or 'Keep quiet'?

Some children have also told us they find it difficult when their parents ask them to get ready for school or when their teachers ask them to do things such as doing some homework or getting changed for sports. Do you find any of these things difficult?

Would you like to write down the demands you find tricky?

- I struggle when my **parents** ask me to:

. . . .

. . . .

- I struggle when my **teachers** ask me to:

....

....

....

- I struggle when **other people** (you can write their names here if you want) ....

....

....

ask me to:

....

....

....

You *can* do it! You *can't* do it!

Some people with PDA have tried to explain to us **how it feels when they are asked to do something that they are perfectly able to do.** Some explained that it felt like if they had two voices inside of their heads arguing with each other: one telling them that they *can* do it and the other telling them that they absolutely *can't*. They explained that this voice telling them not to do something can become very loud and controlling and it is exhausting to try to ignore this voice. Some explain that this voice ordering them not to do something can at times *paralyse* them, stopping them from doing what they want to and can do.

☐ Have you ever experienced anything like this?

It is indeed very tricky to put into words what goes on inside your head when confronted by demands. Feel free to do a drawing to explain this if you prefer to use images rather than words. If you want to do so now or later on, please do it here. It would be really useful for everyone to understand how hard some demands are for you.

Why can't I just do it!?

You might have felt that although **you have the skills to do something** you are asked to do – for example putting your shoes on to get out of the house – **at times, you just can't get yourself to do it**. This can be very frustrating.

☐ Do you often feel this way?

☐ If this is the case, do you feel at a loss to understand why you cannot do it, let alone explain it to others?

• Which are the **requests** you struggle most with?

. . . .

. . . .

. . . .

• Who are the **people** who ask you to do more things that you find it tricky to cooperate with?

. . . .

. . . .

. . . .

What might be making it difficult?

Some young people with PDA have told us that when they are having a bad day, a day when they are feeling stressed out and on edge, they can't do small things that on good days they can manage to do fine.

☐ Does this happen to you?

The young people we have worked with have told us that the following things make it more difficult to meet a demand.

When you've already been trying hard, things are more difficult:

☐ when you feel anxious

☐ when you feel under pressure

☐ when you feel out of control

☐ when you feel on the spot

☐ when you are not given any alternatives

☐ when you are not given a timescale to complete the task

☐ when you are tired

☐ when you are struggling to cope with:
  ☐ noise
  ☐ light
  ☐ smells
  ☐ too many things going on around you
  ☐ someone near you who is getting upset, anxious or excited
  ☐ other things that might be going on, such as:

· ·

Can you think of other circumstances that might make you less able to meet a demand placed on you? You might want to write them here:

· ·

· ·

· ·

· ·

Trying hard to explain the reasons for not being able to do something

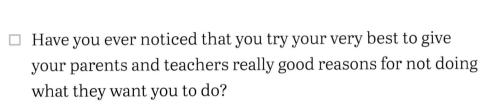

We have observed that young people with PDA often spend a lot of time, effort and energy **explaining to those asking them to do something why they can't do it.**

☐ Have you ever noticed that you try your very best to give your parents and teachers really good reasons for not doing what they want you to do?

My feelings about demands

Trying to survive a world full of demands may feel really tricky and at times impossible. These are frequent feelings we have found in the young people with PDA that we have met.

As you see, the list of feelings we have come up with is rather long, as PDA affects people in different ways. It would be helpful to know **which ones** might apply to you and also **how much** these feelings apply to you on a scale from 0 to 10 (0 meaning that it doesn't apply to you at all and 10 meaning that it does an awful lot).

People asking me to do things I feel I am unable to do makes me feel:

paralysed	☐	exhausted	☐
confused	☐	worried	☐
overwhelmed	☐	helpless	☐
anxious	☐	grumpy	☐
fed up	☐	miserable	☐
angry	☐	stressed	☐
afraid	☐	furious	☐

You may want to write any other feelings we have missed:

. . . .

. . . .

. . . .

. . . .

You want to do something but can't get yourself to do it!

You might also struggle to get yourself to do something that **_you_ want to do**, not something that others want you to do: something that you enjoy or even that you are looking forward to very much. You might want to go out of the house to do something that you are excited about but somehow you start questioning your ability to do it and end up getting all worked up.

Let us share with you some examples from the young people with PDA we have worked with. A boy who loves playing with his Xbox told us that sometimes he feels unable to change the game, even when he really wants to play a different game, and has to ask his mother to do it for him. A girl with PDA told us that although she had been excited about going to the zoo for weeks – she loves animals – on the day the visit was planned she couldn't make herself leave the house.

☐ Do you ever feel unable to do something that _you_ want to do?

☐ Do you ask others to do it for you? If this is the case:
    ☐ Who do you ask the most? . . . .

☐ Do you get angry if they don't do it for you straightaway?

You might want to write here about a time when you wanted to do something and couldn't; maybe you could describe what happened:

....

....

....

Making choices can be hard

Some children and young people with PDA have told us that they don't like it when they are asked to do something without being given a choice. However, we have often heard that they were not able to make up their minds when asked to choose for themselves. **Making decisions can be stressful for some people with PDA.**

☐ Do you find making choices very tricky?

☐ Sometimes even choosing between things you like can be hard, like which TV show to watch. Does this happen to you?

Often feeling very anxious

One of the biggest lessons we have learned from spending many hours listening to children and young people with PDA is that **they are very anxious way too often and that their high levels of anxiety are behind many of the difficulties they face.**

We have heard that they are nervous about being asked to do things, even before they are asked to do anything at all. We have been told that not feeling in control of what's happening to them or what other people are doing makes them stressed and edgy.

Other things fuelling the anxiety that many young people with PDA have shared with us are: being taking by surprise by an unexpected event; when people made changes without warning them; and being confronted with new situations or unknown people.

☐ Does this apply to you? Do you often feel very anxious?

☐ When you are feeling anxious, do you struggle to relax?

The **main triggers** for my anxiety levels to go up are:

. . . .

. . . .

. . . .

We have also learned that sometimes it can be very tricky to identify the trigger for your levels of anxiety to increase, no matter how hard you try to find out the cause.

☐ At times I have **no idea** why my anxiety escalates.

Identifying when you are starting to feel anxious: *The sparks*

It is important for you and for people around you to be able to identify **when you are *starting* to feel anxious so you and others can *stop* the anxiety going up and up**.

Some young people with PDA have found the following image useful to explain the importance of identifying early signs of anxiety in order to stop it from getting out of control: **it is easier to put out a campfire than a forest fire**.

Let us explain what we mean by this: when anxiety starts it is like a small campfire but it can build quickly and become overwhelming like a forest fire. It is then much harder to get the fire under control. If you notice the sparks then it is much easier to put them out than the real forest fire. The same goes for anxiety: you might start to identify early signs of anxiety in your body and your mind (the sparks) and be able to put in place the strategies that work for you to calm down – you will find more about strategies later on in this book. Then you can tell grown-ups what is happening to you so they can help your anxiety to stay at a manageable level (campfire) and not get out of control (forest fire).

You may want to try to think about these important questions

How does anxiety feel in your **body**?

☐ Is it hot?

☐ Is it cold?

☐ Do you shake?

☐ Do you feel numb?

☐ Do you sweat?

☐ Does your breathing become faster?

☐ Does your heart beat faster?

☐ Do you clench your jaw?

Whereabouts in your body do you feel your anxiety building up?
I feel anxiety in my:

☐ stomach

☐ head

☐ throat

☐ heart

☐ legs

☐ hands

☐ any other areas such as:

. . . .

What goes through your **mind** when you are feeling anxious?
What do you **think** is going to happen to you?

These are the **thoughts** racing through my mind when
I'm very anxious:

. . . .

. . . .

Losing control of your actions – your anxiety is the troublemaker

We are very grateful to the young people with PDA who have bravely talked to us about the times when they lost control of their actions. Our work with them made us realise that **what really got out of control in the first place was their levels of anxiety and it was precisely this that made the behaviour become out of control.** In short, it was their anxiety levels going up and up which caused all the trouble!

But don't worry, help is at hand: there is a lot in this book to help you to keep your anxiety manageable, such as the previous pages looking at recognising the early signs of anxiety going up, and lots of strategies in the pages to follow to bring your anxiety down and to keep it down.

☐ When you feel cornered and under pressure, and cannot see a way out of the situation you are in, **do you ever lose control of your actions?**

These times of losing control of your behaviour are really distressing for you and for those caring for you. If you get upset thinking about these times, it might be wise to agree on a time to revisit these pages with the grown-ups you trust the most when you feel more up to it. In our experience, it is best *not* to talk about these difficult times just after they have taken place but when everyone is feeling calmer and more positive.

We would like to stress how important it is that **we all know**

as much as possible about these very difficult times even if we know it is hard to think about them. As our teacher, no one is better equipped than you to tell us about this so we can do our best to help you.

You may want to photocopy and tape up this or any other symbol in the book to point to if words are too much.

How do you lose control?

We have observed **different ways** in which children and young people with PDA react as they are getting increasingly more anxious to the point of losing control of their actions.

You might want to tick the ones applicable to you:

☐ Withdrawing and getting very quiet.

☐ Stopping talking with people when they talk to you.

☐ Using unkind words.

☐ Becoming very angry.

☐ Shouting.

☐ Screaming.

☐ Swearing.

☐ Using shocking language.

☐ Lashing out.

☐ Running away.

☐ Breaking things.

☐ Throwing things.

☐ Disrupting what's going on around you.

☐ Making threats to hurt yourself.

☐ Hurting yourself.

☐ Making threats to hurt others.

☐ Hurting other people.

☐ Other ways such as:

. . . .

. . . .

. . . .

Let us share with you some of the **helpful images** the young people with PDA have used to explain the experience of losing control of their actions.

A boy with PDA drew a **glass full of 'anxiety'** (a liquid he coloured in dark green); the glass was already very full (he found going to school very hard and also struggled with the chaos of his lively younger siblings). He explained that he felt cornered and under pressure to respond to his mother's request to stop playing on the computer as it was dinner time. Having failed to convince her that he couldn't do it, he lost control of his actions by swearing and breaking several objects (he drew the liquid in his glass overflowing and spreading all over the floor).

Other children and young people with PDA have compared the feeling of losing control of their behaviour to a **volcano erupting**: they drew the red-orange lava, which represented their anxiety, building up inside the volcano until the lava couldn't be contained inside anymore and created an explosion with the lava falling everywhere.

Another image a girl with PDA used was that of a **cauldron on a fire** with the food exploding all over the place as the fire – her anxiety – became bigger and bigger (she cleverly wrote on each log she was adding to the fire the trigger for her increasing anxiety such as 'having to wear school uniform' or 'not being allowed to keep her teddy with her at school').

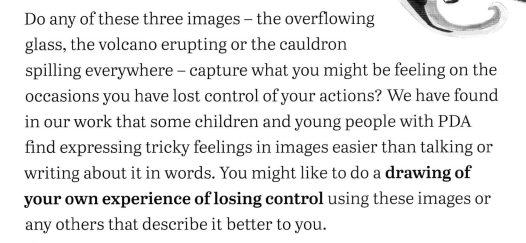

Do any of these three images – the overflowing glass, the volcano erupting or the cauldron spilling everywhere – capture what you might be feeling on the occasions you have lost control of your actions? We have found in our work that some children and young people with PDA find expressing tricky feelings in images easier than talking or writing about it in words. You might like to do a **drawing of your own experience of losing control** using these images or any others that describe it better to you.

If you prefer words rather than pictures, you are welcome to **write about your experiences of losing control**. Here are some questions which you might find helpful to get your writing started but, if you prefer to write freely about your experiences, please jump these questions and do so in the text box on the next page.

- What do your experiences of 'losing control' look like?

. . . .

- How does it make you feel?

. . . .

Some young people with PDA have found it useful to call the times when they lost control by a **nickname**, a name completely different from their own name. For example, a boy with PDA used the name of his neighbour's grumpy dog to refer to these incidents: 'Yesterday, I had a *Rex*.'

- If you would like to give your experience of losing control a nickname, what would it be?

. . . .

- When does . . . . (write the nickname here if you have one) come to visit you?

. . . .

- How often?

. . . .

My experience of losing control:

After losing control

Some young people with PDA have shared with us how they felt once these difficult times of losing control were over. Some explained that they felt **sad and bad about themselves**. Others felt **angry** with those around them – as they believed they had caused it – or with themselves for not having been able to prevent it. While some could describe their feelings quite quickly, for example on the same day, others took longer to be able to explain how they felt.

☐ Does losing control of your actions make you feel sad and bad about yourself?

☐ Does it make you feel angry? If so, with whom?
    ☐ Angry with others?
    ☐ Angry with yourself?

We were also told how much some of them **worried about what other people who had seen them shouting or lashing out thought of them**.

☐ Do you feel particularly bad when you have lost control in front of other people, such as your classmates?

You might want to write down how you feel about these times later on that same day when you have calmed down, or some days later.

Later I felt:

. . . .

. . . .

Not enough time to give you *my* answer!

When we have asked children and young people with PDA if they felt they were given enough time to answer a question, they often replied that they felt that **people moved on to another question too soon before they could fully understand what they were told and were ready to give an answer.**

They often felt rushed to move onto something else when they had not had the chance to say what they wanted to say.

☐ Do you also feel this way? Do you think people often start talking again too soon before you have had time to come up with your answer?

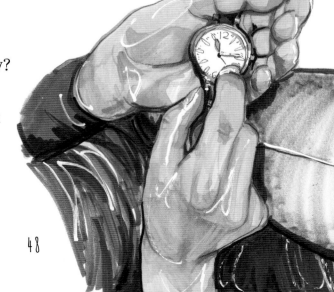

48

Friendships can be tricky

Many of the young people with PDA we
have met are keen to have friends but find
**relationships quite puzzling, tricky
and at times upsetting**. They have told
us that friendships can become sources
of a great deal of anxiety as people can be
unpredictable and their reactions confusing.
If this is the case for you, you may want
to continue exploring more things about
relationships you may find difficult:

☐ Do you feel nervous about how to approach others, how to
talk to them and ask them to be your friend?

☐ Is it difficult to make friends?

☐ Is it difficult to keep friends?

☐ Do you struggle to guess what your friends are going to do
and to understand their reactions?
   ☐ Do you find it hard to guess what others are feeling or
   thinking?
   ☐ Do you find what your classmates do or say quite
   confusing?
   ☐ Do you often think that people are laughing at you but
   are not sure why?

- [ ] Do you get upset if your friends don't do what you want them to do?
  - [ ] Is it much easier to get along with your friends if they follow your lead and follow your rules for the game?
  - [ ] Is it easier to have a shared interest with a friend that you can do together?

- [ ] You might get very upset when things have not worked out as you wished with those you wanted to be friends with:
  - [ ] Do you often feel like your friends are not being good friends?
  - [ ] Do you often feel let down by them?
  - [ ] Do you often feel that they have been unfair, even disloyal to you?

- [ ] You might find that people misunderstand you.
  - [ ] Do people get upset about things you say or do but you don't get why they feel that way?

Is there anything you would like to say to people who misunderstand you?

. . . .

. . . .

. . . .

- [ ] You might prefer to have just one 'special' friend rather than having a group of friends. This friendship that means lots to you may become complicated and upsetting if your friend doesn't want to do what you wish or if they want to be friends with others. We have seen how upsetting this might become for people with PDA.
  - [ ] Do you find being with just one friend easier than being with a group of friends?
  - [ ] If your friend becomes friends with someone else, do you worry your friend is going to stop caring for you?

- [ ] You might find people your own age trickier to get along with. Do you find it easier to get along with:
  - [ ] adults?
  - [ ] younger children?

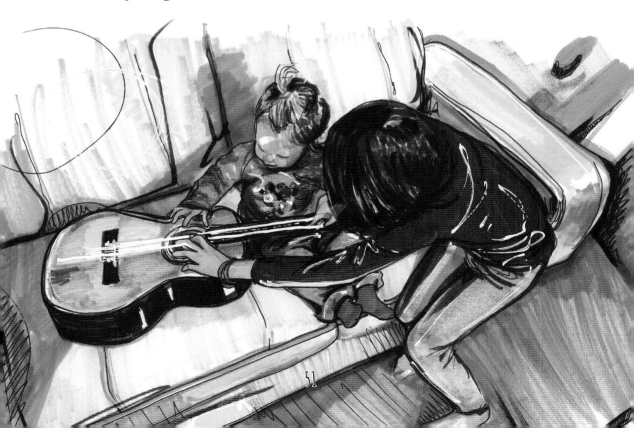

Carried away by my imagination...

We have observed that some young people with PDA have very active imaginations and enjoy doing role-plays, acting and mimicking (Dr Glòria always finds it amusing when some patients of hers have perfectly imitated her Spanish accent!). You might become part of the fantasy world portrayed in a movie, TV series or book. You might find that this fantasy world is not only much more exciting and fun but also easier and safer for you to navigate than real life, as you can learn the rules and predict the characters' reactions because you enjoy spending lots of time watching or reading about them. Some others have told us that they love to spend time with certain toys, for example a special soft toy that becomes very important to them, and that these toys have names and personalities. They find it easier and safer to communicate with these special toys than with real people, and they also keep them company and make them feel less alone.

☐ Do you like taking on different roles of characters in the TV or mimicking people around you?

☐ Do you like to pretend you are a different person or character?

☐ Do you find your fantasy world safer and better than the real world? Do you like to escape to it when you feel stressed or confused?

If you like, you can draw a picture here to illustrate your favourite way to play using your imagination. You may want to draw your favourite toy or fictional character. If you prefer you can draw yourself doing some acting or role-playing, or draw someone you mimic here. Your choice!

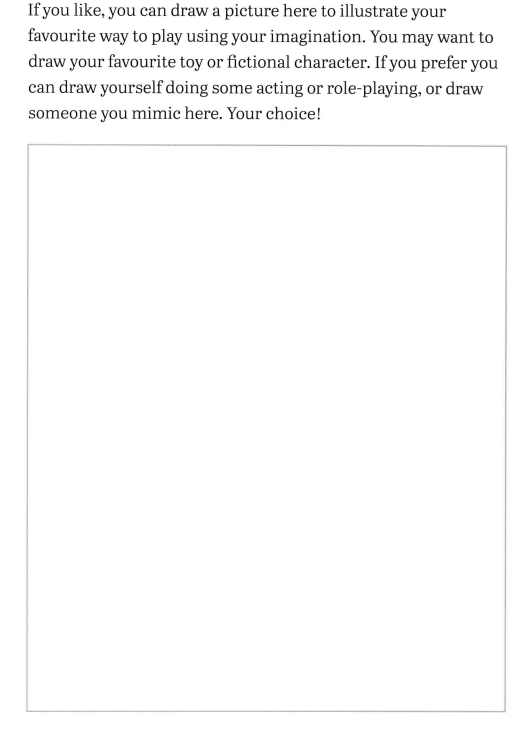

Although using your imagination and acting skills are wonderful things to do, young people with PDA have shared with us times when **their imagination got them in trouble as they were carried away by their fantasy world.**

☐ Have you ever been carried away by your imagination and it all got a bit too much?

If this was the case, it might be useful to explore this a little bit further by looking at these questions:

☐ Do you interact with your toys or characters from video games or films as if they were real?

☐ Do your favourite fictional characters end up taking up too much of your time and you find it tricky to stop thinking or even worrying about them?

☐ Have fantasy and reality ever become confused?

☐ Have your toys ever become too controlling of you or other people around you?

☐ If other people want to join you in your acting and to play a part in your stories, do you get angry with them if they don't stick to your script and follow your lead?

☐ Do you find yourself copying those around you and taking on their roles, interests or personalities?

You might want to tell us about a time when your fantasy world or role-playing might have got you in trouble:

....

....

....

....

....

....

....

Some things occupy my thoughts too much

You might have some things that **take a lot of your time and occupy your thoughts**.

Although these vary from one person to another, most people tend to become very upset when others around them try to question them about their worries and thoughts. For example, some people with PDA might want to follow very strict routines or get very absorbed in one particular activity that they love and get very angry if they are not allowed to get their own way. Others will get very fixated about a certain topic, toy, fictional character or story. Yet others might spend a lot of energy and time in collecting something and will get very cross if their collection is not as complete as they want or if someone touches it. You might also find that you spend a lot of time thinking about a particular person such as a friend, a teacher or a famous person.

☐ Do you spend a lot of time thinking about something or someone?

☐ Do you get upset if someone tries to challenge you about your worries or thoughts?

You might want to write other things that fill your head a lot here:

. . . .

....

....

....

Or, you might want to draw a picture of the kind of things that fill your head:

Struggling to go to school

Children and young people with PDA often **worry about going to school and find it tricky to get ready in the mornings.** Some struggle so much that they fail to attend school. If going to school is hard for you too, you might want to have a look at the following questions so we can learn about this difficulty:

- ☐ When do you worry the most about going to school?
  - ☐ In the mornings while getting ready.
  - ☐ At bedtime on a week day thinking about having school the following morning.

- ☐ Does worrying about school interfere with your sleep?
  - ☐ On Sundays worrying about the week ahead.
  - ☐ Coming to the end of a holiday period.

- ☐ Is it a struggle to get ready in the mornings to get to school on time? Is it so bad that:
  - ☐ you are often late for school?
  - ☐ you sometimes miss school?

58

☐ Does the journey to school make you anxious?

☐ Is it difficult to leave school at the end of the day to go home?

☐ Some children with PDA have told us that they particularly struggle with specific aspects of their school timetable like:
  ☐ sports
  ☐ lunch times
  ☐ break times
  ☐ school trips
  ☐ exams
  ☐ assemblies
  ☐ concerts, plays and shows.

Here we have written down some of the **reasons** we were given when we asked children with PDA why going to school was hard for them. Maybe you've noticed some of these too:

☐ Do you find learning difficult?

☐ Is concentrating at school tricky?

☐ Do you often find that completing the tasks the teacher sets you is very hard?

☐ Do you worry about not fitting in with your classmates and about not having friends?

☐ Do you find the day at school exhausting?
  ☐ Does this exhaustion from school mess up your evening at home?
  ☐ Do you feel more on edge at home after a difficult day at school?
  ☐ Do you like to retreat to your bedroom after school to chill out doing your favourite hobby?

☐ Do you often feel confused at school, not knowing what you are supposed to be doing?

☐ Do you feel that other pupils learn and do homework easily when you find it very hard?
  ☐ Does this make you angry?
  ☐ Does this make you feel bad about yourself?

☐ When you have completed a piece of homework or learned a lesson, do you still feel that is not good enough and give yourself a hard time?

☐ Do you worry about unexpected changes happening in your school, such as an activity being cancelled or a teacher you particularly like being sick?

You might want to write here any **other things** you struggle with at school that we have missed:

. . . .

. . . .

. . . .

. . . .

Puzzled about feelings

We have covered here quite a lot about some of the struggles young people with PDA have shared with us. We would like to end this section on difficulties with some final reflections we have got from young people with PDA about **how puzzling and even troubling their feelings can become at times.** You might want to have a look at them to see if they are also true for you.

- ☐ Do you find it very tricky to know how you are feeling? Do you find yourself at a loss to answer questions about what's going on inside you?

- ☐ Some young people with PDA have explained that they seem to feel very happy about things or incredibly unhappy and that there is nothing in the middle. Do you also feel this way?

We have already talked about how hard coping with things that make you anxious can be for you, but how about things that make you very excited? Some people with PDA have described that they also **find managing activities that they are actually very much looking forward to tricky**.

- ☐ Do you ever struggle to cope with things that make you super thrilled as it can get all a bit too overwhelming for you to cope with?

☐ Do you get very impatient about waiting to do the things you enjoy? Has not coping with the waiting ended up spoiling it all for you?

We have been told by people with PDA that at particularly anxious times they feel that they have **no control over the way they act and feel**. A girl with PDA we know called these times as entering her **'robotic mode'**, as she explained that she felt like she was becoming a robot that was programmed to act automatically without any alternative choice. She described to us that, when she became her robot version, she felt urged to do things that she could not stop.

☐ Do you often feel so rushed to do something that you feel you cannot control your actions?

☐ At these times, do you feel so rushed that you feel that you have no time you can possibly spare to think about the consequences of your actions?

This girl also used the image of her becoming her robot version to explain the sudden changes in the way she felt, which she thought to be at times outside her control. Parents and those looking after children and young people with PDA have told us that they have observed that children with PDA **can go from one extreme of the feeling spectrum to the other at great speed.**

We have suggested before that it can be helpful to rate your feelings from 0 to 10 (0 meaning that it doesn't apply to you at all and 10 meaning that it does an awful lot) so you can gradually become more aware of your feelings. Also, you can see that there are other options regarding the intensity of your feelings rather than just the extremes (0 and 10).

- ☐ Have you noticed that you can go very fast from feeling very distressed to completely cool? Or the opposite: from relaxed to very upset in a flash?

- ☐ Do you feel that these changes in the way you feel are sometimes so sudden and quick that they are outside of your control?

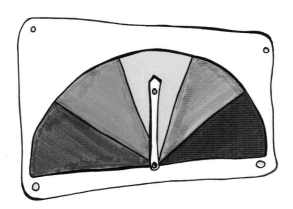

Your Own Strategies to Help Tackle Your Challenges

After going through the difficulties, at last here you have **some strategies that children and young people with PDA have told us they find useful to help them face their difficulties and to cope with day-to-day demands.**

What if you continue role-playing the **teacher** and tell us which of these strategies work for you, so we can learn how to help you best?

It would be really useful to create **a list of strategies decided by you that truly work for you that everyone around you knows about and can use.**

Give me options

Young people with PDA have often complained to us of feeling bossed around by others as if they had no escape or choice.

Some people with PDA have told us that, when they are asked to do something, **being given a choice really helps them and makes them less anxious**, as they feel more in control.

☐ Do you find it helpful to be given options for you to choose from when you are asked to do something?

Give me options *but keep in mind...*

Although being given choices can indeed be helpful for some people with PDA, not everyone has the same preferences regarding how they would like this to be done.

Some children with PDA have told us that they struggle if they are given too many options to choose from as it can get too confusing: what they find most helpful is to be given just **two simple options to choose from, that are clearly explained to them, with plenty of time** to come up with a decision. Many people with PDA struggle if they feel under pressure to make a choice. For example, if they feel rushed or are put on the spot to decide.

- ☐ Is it easier to be given just two options which are clearly explained to you?

- ☐ Do you need to be given lots of time to decide which option to go for?

- ☐ Does it help to check out the good and bad parts of each choice with someone?

- ☐ Is it easier to make a choice when the options are written down for you?

- ☐ Do you find it easier to make a choice when the options are presented as images, so you can pick the image you want to go for?

- ☐ Is it better to be asked about making a decision when you are on your own and not in front of others, for example not in front of your classmates?

It is important to remember that, although many young people with PDA like to be offered an alternative when asked to do something, **there are others who find making choices difficult** even when they like all the choices they are given. Is this your case?

- ☐ Do you find making choices stressful?

People with PDA who normally prefer to be given options to choose from can at times find the whole thing of making up their minds way too much. We have learned from young people with PDA, and from those teaching and looking after them, that **if making a decision is becoming too hard, stressful, and is taking too long, the best thing to do is to move on to something else and to go back to making the choice later on when everyone is feeling more relaxed and positive about it.** Also, when things are feeling very out of control, being given choices might not be enough to help. In such cases, it might be best to leave it aside for the time being and wait to try again when you are feeling calmer. **It will be done when it can be done.**

☐ If making a choice is getting too stressful, do you prefer to drop the whole thing and go back to it later on when you feel ready?

Having a 'safe space'

Many young people with PDA have told us that having a 'safe space' is terribly important for them. What do they mean by this? **A 'safe space' is a place that they can go to when they are feeling anxious and when everything is becoming too much.** They highlighted how useful having such a place is for them, especially at school. It is worthwhile to ask your teachers to help you to identify your 'safe space' at school and how to signal that you need to go there. There are many ways to let your teacher know that you need to go to your 'safe space', for example, showing them a red piece of card. It is also important to agree on who will be keeping an eye on you while you are in your 'safe space' or even who will be with you all the time, if it was not safe to leave you alone. Your 'safe space' should be your choice as much as possible so you can really feel safe and in control.

Having a place to go when you are becoming more and more anxious and are starting to fear that you may even lose control will help you to **slowly calm down so you gradually feel back in control of yourself**. If you were to lose control, you would be in a safe and private space cared for by grown-ups who know how to help you and not in front of other people, such as in front of your classmates.

☐ Do you have a 'safe space'?

☐ Would you like to tell us about your 'safe space'?
    ☐ At home it's . . . .
    ☐ At school it's . . . .
    ☐ Any other 'safe space' you may have: . . . .

If you don't have a 'safe space' yet, would you like to write some options here? You can then show them to your parents and teachers so you can all agree on your very own 'safe space' at home and at school:

. . . .

. . . .

. . . .

What can you do in your 'safe space'?

Would you like to imagine you are in your 'safe space'? What can you do there?

Let's try to relax: doing anything that helps you to chill out would be a good idea. Any activity that absorbs and distracts you and takes your mind away from what

is bothering you is a good activity to do in your 'safe space'. Go for it!

Here you have some of the strategies the children and young people with PDA we work with use in their 'safe spaces'. Remember that relaxation strategies are very personal and what someone finds soothing and calming, another may find stressful. You might want to tick the activities that have worked to calm you down in the past or those that you think might work for you, so you can give them a try.

☐ Your hobbies, which are:

. . . .

. . . .

. . . .

. . . .

. . . .

☐ Playing sports (your 'safe space' can be an open space like a garden).

☐ Breathing exercises.

☐ Yoga exercises.

☐ Listening to music.

☐ Playing an instrument.

☐ Drawing.

Some children have found learning a few breathing and yoga exercises useful. You might want to role-play that you are a yoga teacher and teach the grown-up who is with you in your 'safe space' some of those techniques.

Maybe you can write here any other relaxing activity that works for you:

. . . .

. . . .

. . . .

. . . .

If you can't access your 'safe space' for whatever reason you can also pretend you are in it using your imagination or you can try to find an alternative one in which to use your relaxation strategies. For example, a young boy with PDA, who was getting very worked up in the supermarket, cleverly managed to create a 'safe space' in his mother's car. You may want to think with your parents about which alternative 'safe spaces' you can use when you are out and about, or even agree beforehand about 'safe spaces' you can go to when you are on holiday or visiting a relative.

My **alternative 'safe spaces'** are:

. . . .

. . . .

. . . .

How about drawing a picture of yourself in your **'safe space'**? Wouldn't it be nice to draw yourself becoming all chilled out and happy while doing your favourite relaxing activity?

Having a 'safe person'

It is as important to have a 'safe person' as it is to have a 'safe space'.

A 'safe person' is someone you can go to when things are getting too much and you are becoming upset. Your 'safe person' is there to help you calm down and regain control.

Your 'safe person' can be with you in your 'safe space' so you feel doubly safe.

It is good to have more than one 'safe person', as you are not always in the same place, and one 'safe person' may not be available. It is better to talk about your 'safe people' or a 'safety team'.

My 'safe people':

☐ My 'safe person/people' at home is/are:

. . . .

☐ My 'safe person/people' at school is/are:

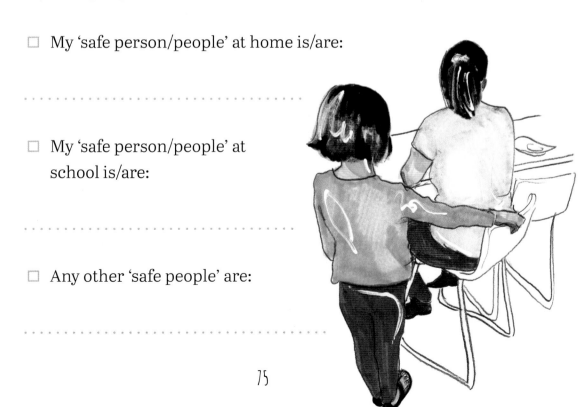

. . . .

☐ Any other 'safe people' are:

. . . .

You've been doing such a great job teaching us about your own PDA! Your 'safe people' are your special pupils, the ones keenest to learn from you.

Would you like to draw your **'safe person'** or **'safe people'**? If so, you can do it here. If you like, you can also draw yourself teaching these special pupils about which things they can do to help you to relax or doing an activity with them that makes you feel better.

Being in control of my plans and routines

We have been told by many children with PDA how much they struggle when others decide for them and that they find it much easier when they feel in control of what is happening to them. They explained how important **having clear routines and plans is for them as it makes them feel safe and in control**. This way they can stop worrying about unexpected events taking them by surprise.

They also told us, loud and clear, three things about their routines for everyone to keep in mind: first, that **they want to be part of designing their plans and routines as much as possible**; second, **to be given lots of warning if there are going to be any changes** and third, they warned us that **there needs to be room for flexibility in their routines so changes and adaptations can be made if they are having a trying day** (for example, opting out of some of the more challenging activities in their plans on those days).

How about you and your routines?

☐ Is it easier when you know your routines and plans very well?

☐ When your timetable at school and your activities at home are designed just for you, and you have given input in coming up with them, do you feel calmer?

☐ Is it easier to be given lots of warning if there are going to be any changes in your plans and routines?

☐ When having one of those trickier days, do you need to be allowed to make changes in your routines to make the day easier?

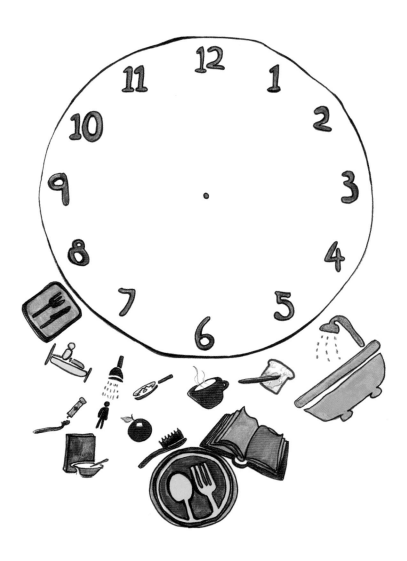

My most important routines

Being happy with the morning and bedtime routines is very important as they happen every day. There's a space to write a morning and bedtime routine here. This way, everyone will know the steps you take in getting ready in the morning and at night time. It may be useful to be detailed and even to draw some pictures to illustrate the different things you do at every step, if you prefer to. It may be better to use a pencil, so you can rub it out later, as routines can change with time.

My morning routine

These are the steps I follow when I wake up in the morning (you may want to number them in the order you carry out the steps: 1, 2, 3, etc.):

My bedtime routine

These are the steps I take before getting into bed (you may want to number them in the order you carry out the steps: 1, 2, 3, etc.):

....

....

....

....

....

....

....

....

....

....

....

....

....

....

....

....

Other important routines

Besides your morning and bedtime routines, you may have
other routines that are important to you (for example, the
routine you follow to get to school or the timetable that you
follow at school). You may want to detail any other important
routines you have here using words or drawings or both.

....

....

....

....

....

We have learned from children and young people with PDA about **the importance of getting them involved when making up their routines and plans**. Taking into account their preferences and listening to their concerns are key aspects of coming up with a successful routine or plan.

We have seen again and again the **positive difference that changing a particularly troublesome step or steps in a routine can make, especially when the change is led by the child or young person themselves**.

So, how about if you were to tell the grown-ups caring for you about any changes you'd like to make to your routines? **Any change that can make following your routines easier for you is worth considering.** You can also ask for times to be adjusted or for the order of the steps to change. You can put images next to what you prefer to happen at different times of the day. For example, you might want to give your morning shower a miss and to have an evening bath instead.

- Things I'd like to change in my **morning routine:**

....

....

....

....

....

....

- Things I'd like to change in my **bedtime routine:**

....

....

....

....

....

....

- Things I'd like to change in my **other important routines**:

．．

．．．

．．．

．．．

．．．

．．．

．．．

．．．

．．．

So now, how about if you have a think with your parents and teachers about these changes that you want? If some of them are possible, you may like to go back to the previous pages where you have detailed these routines and make the changes you have agreed. Then it becomes official and everyone knows about these very important changes that are going to make things easier for you.

My 'ideal time'

If something is ideal it means it is the best possible option. **An 'ideal time' is a time just for you to do what makes you feel happy and chilled out.** No demands or expectations attached to this time!

We all need to have times to follow our very own 'ideal time'. Enjoying our 'ideal time' helps us to recharge and have the energy to put up with our other not-so-ideal times.

You can certainly have more than one 'ideal time' activity. In fact the more ideal activities you have the better. So if you can't do one for whatever reason (for example, your 'ideal time' is playing in the park and it is raining a lot), you have other great plans you can do instead.

'Ideal time' is very personal and varies from one person to the next. For example, for a boy with PDA we worked with – who was finding going to school hard and tiring – his 'ideal time' was on a Saturday and consisted of staying in his bedroom most of the day, in pyjamas and playing with his Xbox. The 'ideal time' for a girl with PDA we met – who was very fond of animals – was to spend an afternoon a week in a local farm caring for the animals.

88

My very own super 'ideal time' activity

If you want to, you can write or draw your 'ideal time' activity or activities here. You might want to use a pencil, as your ideal activity can change with time: your favourite 'ideal time' activity today can look very different in a year's time.

....

....

....

It is important to find time to carry out the ideal activity or activities you've drawn or written about above. Weekends and evenings can be good times. Why don't you spend some time thinking with your parents about which might be good times to schedule your ideal activity?

These are the times for my ideal activity to take place:

....

....

....

....

Feeling cornered and about to lose control...

Young people with PDA have told us that when they feel under lots of pressure and backed into a corner, their anxiety might reach such high levels that they lose control of their actions. **It would be great if those situations could be reduced in frequency and severity as much as possible**

as we have witnessed how distressing these times are. Several pages in the challenges section were devoted to exploring such times, your reactions and how you felt during and after them.

How can *you* help *yourself?* How can *others* help *you?*

Now, in your role as our teacher, you might want to teach us which strategies work for you to cope better during those times that you are feeling cornered and about to lose control of your behaviour. Or, even better, to teach us ways to avoid getting to those times in which your anxiety levels are so high that you are likely to lose control.

Sharing with us specific things that you and others can do to help prevent and manage those times better is incredibly useful information.

'Danger zone'...'point of no return'...

A young person with PDA we worked with used the term **'danger zone'** to describe the time before losing control when he was getting more and more worked up, with his anxiety levels increasing rapidly as he was getting close to losing it. He called the **'point of no return'** the precise moment of losing control of his actions.

Acting early!

These terms express really well the **importance of acting during the 'danger zone' and if possible, to avoid altogether getting there in the first place**. Moreover, once in the 'danger zone', some children with PDA can very quickly reach the 'point of no return', not leaving much time to put many strategies in place.

This is why it is so very important for you and those caring for you to **detect the early signs that you might be approaching the 'danger zone', and if you are already there, not to spare any efforts to get you out as soon as possible**.

Once you get past the point of no return, you are feeling so out of control that it is unlikely you can effectively use calming strategies. Besides keeping you and others safe, there is not much for those caring for you left to do either but for everyone to wait for you to calm down and regain control.

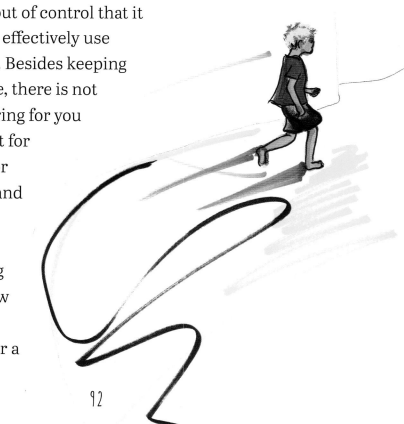

To make answering the questions below easier, it might be useful to remember a time when you lost control of your behaviour. We know this is not an easy thing to do, so it is important that you tackle these questions when you are feeling calm and up to it.

While at times it is obvious what made you lose control of your actions, we also know that at other times it is not easy for you and those around you to be able to find the cause. These cases in which there are no apparent causes are rather puzzling: once it is all over, you and everyone else are left wondering what it was all about as you seemed fine just before.

Well, good teachers do like challenges! Getting back to your role-playing as the teacher, you might want to explain to us what it's like **just before entering the 'danger zone'** and what was going on inside and outside of you. You are the best one to explain what it's like **inside** you!

It might be useful for you to remember that it takes time to work things out: sometimes you can only work things out by talking to someone, or by learning more about feelings through experience. Feelings can be difficult to understand and explain: the great thing is that as you become gradually aware of your feelings, you make better sense to yourself and may then even help those around you to understand your feelings too. Sometimes, describing your feelings in words or pictures can be helpful too.

So, let's try to remember a time when you lost control of your behaviour. Can you think of the **trigger or triggers** for you to lose control?

....

....

....

Were there any **warning signs** that you were entering the 'danger zone'? Were there any changes in the way you behaved, in the way you felt? What was going through your mind?

....

....

....

Knowing the main causes and being alert to your warning signs are very valuable bits of information as you and those caring for you can prevent these situations from happening or progressing by putting in place the relaxation strategies that you have been teaching us. **Acting early, as soon as you feel your anxiety is spiralling up, is incredibly**

important to prevent these distressing incidents. It is useful to remember from before that **your high levels of anxiety are the ones causing trouble and making your behaviour get out of control.**

In the 'danger zone'

What can you and others do when you are already in the 'danger zone'? How about trying to put in place any **strategies that help you to relax**, so your anxiety levels stop going up and up? The purpose of these strategies is to **stop you approaching the 'point of no return'** and give you time to find your way out of the 'danger zone'. You have already taught us lots about your preferred relaxation strategies; let's remind ourselves of some here:

How can **you** help yourself while in your 'danger zone'?

- ☐ Going to your 'safe space'.

- ☐ Asking your 'safe person' for help.

- ☐ Breathing exercises.

- ☐ Trying to distract yourself, for example, doing something that you like and chills you out.

- ☐ Doing your hobbies.

Any other activities that work well for you:

. . . .

. . . .

How can your **parents/teachers/important adults** help you while in your danger zone?

☐ I prefer to be left alone to calm down.

☐ I prefer . . . .
(please write the name or names) to be with me:
  ☐ without talking to me or fussing over me
  ☐ reassuring me in the following way: . . . .

. . . .

☐ Other ways you would like to be helped during these times:

· ·

Past the 'point of no return'

When this line has been crossed and you are in the middle of experiencing full-blown anxiety and have lost control, there is not much you can do to help yourself. Those caring for you are there to keep you and others safe.

Is there anything else that you might find it useful for **others** to do?

· ·

· ·

· ·

· ·

· ·

· ·

Regaining control of yourself

Once your anxiety is starting to lessen and you are feeling more in control:

- What would **you** like to do?

....

....

....

....

....

- What would you like **others** to do?

....

....

....

....

....

Thinking afterwards

It might be useful to look back at the times when you have lost control of your behaviour, not immediately after, but when some time has gone by. A few days are often needed for you and those caring for you to be able to do this. We know that it is not an easy task at all, but learning from these experiences can certainly be worthwhile.

- What could **grown-ups** have done differently to avoid it?

....

....

....

....

....

- What could **you** have done differently to avoid it?

....

....

....

....

....

I am very sensitive to...

Young people with PDA can be very sensitive to certain things such as smells and noise. We have learned that **it is very important that sensory needs are taken into account**, as not doing so makes coping much more difficult. They have also shared with us that too much going on at the same time, too much stimulation, can be very unpleasant and may led to feeling distressed and unable to manage. This is called **sensory overload.**

I am very sensitive to:

☐ smells

☐ too much noise

☐ materials

☐ people touching me

☐ light

☐ tastes

☐ texture of foods

☐ other things we have missed:

Everyone needs to know about the ticks you have just made as it is very likely that your anxiety goes up when people are not aware of these difficulties.

☐ Do you feel calmer and more able to cope when allowances are made for your specific sensory needs?

It is really worthwhile to take the time to make the necessary changes to address your being extra sensitive to certain things. For example, Dr Glòria learned that a little boy with PDA was struggling with the lights and the feeling of the sofa in her office. Just remembering to switch off the electric lights – enough light was coming through the windows – and throwing a nice soft blanket over the sofa made all the difference to her patient.

How would you like your parents and teachers to help you with friendships?

Children and young people with PDA have often told us that they want to have friends and have often complained of feeling lonely, but somehow relationships can be really confusing and even upsetting for them. Having friends to have a good time with could help you to feel happier and can also help you to not become too absorbed in your special interest or fantasy world.

You may welcome **help from your parents and teachers to develop and maintain good friendships.** These are some of the things that we have seen work for children and young people with PDA. Do you like any of these ideas?

☐ Helping you to be included in other people's activities.

☐ Assisting you to understand others' reactions when they become confusing.

☐ Helping you to become more confident with your peers by, for example, practising some ways to approach and talk to someone else at school.

☐ Helping to explain to others which aspects of friendships you find tricky, for example, that you may need to be given quite a long time to really trust someone.

☐ Finding shared interests for you and a friend to do together.

Inviting a friend over to your house or to do an activity together outdoors while having your parents on hand can prove helpful as they will be nearby if things don't go according to plan.

☐ Would you like your parents to be on hand in case your meeting with a friend doesn't go well?

What other ways might work for you? Are there any other ways that have worked in the past?

. . . .

. . . .

. . . .

. . . .

. . . .

. . . .

Please make my learning fun and original

You may get bored of being asked by grown-ups to do your school work in the same way again and again. We have observed that some children with PDA respond better to learning when it is led by them as much as possible, for example, choosing which task to do first. Also, they much prefer it when teachers make their lessons fun and original. Is this the case with you too?

☐ Have you noticed that when you are asked to do something that is new, creative and exciting, you find it easier to do it?

☐ Is learning easier if you can do it in a practical way through the things you enjoy doing? For example, doing a treasure hunt to discover and learn the different lines of a poem.

☐ Do you prefer to be given a choice of subjects or projects rather than having this decided for you?

Let's use my imagination in my learning

You might have found – or be willing to give it a go – that **using your imagination and role-play skills can be useful to learn new things and to manage some tasks.** These are a few of the many ways children with PDA have told us they use their wonderful imagination to assist them in their learning. Let's see if any of this works or could work for you:

- ☐ Is it easier to learn if your teacher uses your special toy, a puppet or a fictional character from a story you like to teach you?

- ☐ Do you find it easier to learn if you are teaching others, for example, playing the role of the teacher?

- ☐ Do you enjoy acting the content of a lesson as a mini theatre production?

- ☐ Have you tried applying your drawing skills, turning your lessons into images or comics?

- ☐ Have you tried to use your writing skills, turning your lessons into stories?

Please write here any other ways you could use your imagination to help you with your learning:

. . . .

Using my imagination for lots of things

It might be worth remembering that **your vivid imagination can be an excellent tool, not just for learning, but for lots of other things** such as to relax, to complete rather boring tasks or even to get through a doctor's appointment you may be wary of...just to mention a few.

Let us share with you two examples from Dr Glòria's

practice that you may like: a girl with PDA successfully laid the table for dinner at home most evenings by imagining herself to be a waitress in an exotic restaurant (the country the restaurant was in, its style and the guests varied according to her imagination).

Or the case of a young boy with PDA who found it much easier to attend his appointments with Dr Glòria by bringing his special soft toy animal – a panda – to be the patient and for him to play the psychiatrist who asked questions to the toy. He obligingly translated the answers of his toy to Dr Glòria, who at times was allowed to play the junior doctor in training or a relative of the toy, even once being instructed to be his secretary.

Praise me but do it *my way!*

Some people with PDA struggle when others give them a compliment, praise them in public and make a fuss about them.

☐ Do you find compliments difficult to handle?

☐ When you are praised about something good you have done, do you ever feel that people are going to expect you to behave like that all the time and this makes you anxious?

☐ Does it make you feel nervous to be the centre of attention when you are praised in public?

If you have not ticked any of these three questions, the content of this page is not for you, so please jump to the next section. But if you have, then please let us all know how you would prefer people to compliment and praise you so we can take note!

- [ ] Do you prefer to overhear a compliment directed to you? For example, to hear your teacher telling another teacher how good you have been.

- [ ] Is it better when people write down praise about you for you to read it when you feel like it, when no one else is around?

- [ ] What if others, as well as you, were told you've all done really well? For example, your teacher might say that the whole class has been great.

- [ ] Rather than being told verbally or in writing how well you have done, do you prefer to be given a specific reward, for example giving you extra time to do something you really enjoy such as playing with a favourite toy?

- [ ] Is it better if what you have done well is praised rather than the fact of you doing it? For example, 'I love the way the drawing was done'?

How do you like your information?

You might appreciate it when the people around you interact with you in a **clear, unfussy and straightforward way**. Some people with PDA that we have met have told us that **they don't like to be rushed to respond** to people. It might also be important for you to **be given plenty of time** to consider what you have been told before responding and for people to make sure you are ready to move on to talking about something else.

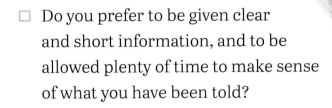

☐ Do you prefer to be given clear and short information, and to be allowed plenty of time to make sense of what you have been told?

☐ Do you find it easier when information is presented as pictures?

☐ Do you find it very annoying and also confusing when you are given too much information?

My 'tailor-made' description of PDA

Job done! You have come to the end of your exploration into the things you struggle with and the strategies that are right for you.

It could be good to write down in the following summary pages all the difficulties and strategies that you have ticked before so you have only those applicable to you in one place.

These pages are a description of what PDA means for you and the best ways to help you. They are not a 'general description' of PDA but **your very own tailor-made description of how PDA affects you**. We like the term 'tailor-made' to describe these summary pages. 'Tailor-made' means made to fit you exactly: when you buy a shirt in a shop, you just have a few sizes available to you – for example: small, medium and large – but a tailor will take the exact measures of your chest, your arms, and so on, so the shirt fits you perfectly. Your shirt is unique to you. In the same way, **these summary pages are unique to you**.

These pages can be photocopied and shared with the important adults around you so they learn how to help you best. By sharing these pages with them, remember that you are **their teacher**, showing them what you have discovered about your PDA and the ways to get around your challenges.
Ready to start writing your 'tailor-made' description of PDA? You will find below the main areas children and young people with PDA struggle with and the main strategies they use to cope with them that we have included in the book. Following each difficulty and strategy, there is a free writing space to summarise your very own findings about them: the most important things you have learned in the previous pages.

   Obviously, we are only

interested in the difficulties and strategies you have identified that are applicable to you: the ones you have ticked and the ones that we've missed and you added. Any of the points below that are not true for you, please leave the writing space blank or write 'Not me!' or something along those lines so we all know that they don't fit you.

You may be up for doing this summarising and writing yourself: if this is the case, go for it! However, if you are feeling tired after the exploration into your PDA, you may prefer to ask one of the important grown-ups around you – such as your parents or a teacher – to do the summarising and writing for you. We are sure they will be more than happy to oblige!

MY DIFFICULTIES: The things I struggle with

- I struggle to cooperate with demands: being asked to do things makes me often feel incredibly anxious.

- Making choices can be hard: choosing between things can become stressful for me.

- I feel very anxious way too often and calming down when I feel this way is tricky.

- When I feel cornered and under a lot of pressure, with my anxiety going up and up, I am likely to lose control of my actions.

- I am often not given enough time to answer: I feel that people move on to another question too soon before I've had a chance to have a say.

- I find friendships quite puzzling, tricky and at times upsetting.

- My imagination sometimes gets me in trouble as I can get carried away by my fantasy world.

- There are some things that occupy my thoughts too much.

- I struggle to go to school: school-related stuff is a great source of anxiety and distress.

- Making sense of my feelings is difficult: my feelings can become rather confusing, muddled-up and even cause trouble if I am unable to control them.

- Please write here any other difficulty you have that we have not included.

MY STRATEGIES: What works for me

- Being given a choice helps me as it makes me feel more in control and less anxious.

- Having 'safe spaces' at home and at school is a must.

- Having 'safe people' around me is a top priority.

- Having a say in my plans and routines is terribly important for me.

- Feeling cornered and about to lose control: these are the ways I and others can help.

- Taking into account my sensory needs is vital.

- I welcome the following help from the important adults in my life to make friendships easier and more enjoyable.

- I find it easier to learn if learning is made fun, original and exciting, and if I am allowed to use my imagination.

- My imagination is an excellent tool not just for learning but for the following other things:

- Being praised makes me feel good but only if you do it in the following way:

- I like my information to be given to me in a clear, straightforward and unfussy way.

- Please add here any other strategy that works for you that we have missed.

Here is another letter.
It could be called The Epilogue.
This means it's near the end of the book.

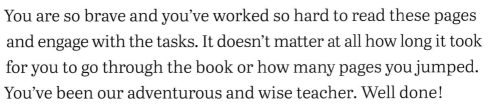

Goodbye Letter to You

Dear Reader,

You are so brave and you've worked so hard to read these pages and engage with the tasks. It doesn't matter at all how long it took for you to go through the book or how many pages you jumped. You've been our adventurous and wise teacher. Well done!

When you have gone through the book once, you're going to want to take a break. But when you've had a good long break **you might want to revisit this book,** to have a look at what you ticked, wrote and drew in it. It might be something you revisit many times. The more you read it and talk about it with your family and teachers the more it will become familiar and less scary and **you will become better and better at explaining it to others and at putting into practice the strategies** you've learned that work for you. It's so important to share it with those around you so they can understand you better and can give you the help that is right for you. **As you grow and develop more skills, difficulties will be overcome.** This is why it might be a good idea for you to use pencil at the beginning of the book because you can erase those difficulties you have overcome. You might even find new strategies that you want to add.

We are confident that you, and those who care about you, are going to find ways to help you achieve your goals and to lead a happy life.

All the very best,

Glòria and *Tamar*

Here is a goodbye letter from us to your parents.

Dear Parents,

Although knowledge of PDA is still at an early stage, **we are excited and optimistic about the future** as we are witnessing how more research projects are being set up to increase our understanding, and more individualised programmes are being developed to respond to the specific needs of the child with these difficulties. We are also sure that you are going to continue with the fantastic task of being the advocates for your child. Supported by professionals, we are confident that you will carry on fostering their skills, helping them to gain insights into their emotions, develop adaptive coping strategies and find ways to gradually increase their tolerance to requests: above all, enabling them to enjoy their life. **We hope this book will be an aid and an ally in your journey to help your child to gain more self-awareness.**

This book was written for your child to learn their very own strategies. Although this is indeed not a manual for parents and professionals – we recommend the manual written by Phil Christie and colleagues which can be found on the 'books of related interest' page – you are also going to learn many new ways to support your child and to manage their behaviour by accompanying them in the process of identifying their difficulties and finding their own strategies to cope with them. Having said that, we cannot stop ourselves from sharing a few practical tips we have seen that have made a difference in our work with parents of children who exhibit PDA patterns of behaviour, and to do so in a simple and easy way to remember by using an acronym. At times, finding the right approach to support your child may have ended up feeling as hard as having to 'find a needle in a haystack'; well rather than a 'needle', a 'pin', as **'find a pin'** is the acronym that contains the initials for the recommendations we would like to leave you with.

F: is for having a **Flexible** approach – basically all the time! Tasks will need to be adjusted to how anxious your child is feeling, and their levels of anxiety can change very quickly and very often. Also, being flexible and creative in the way you engage your child to do something that they might find tricky: using a fun, creative and attractive manner can work wonders. The tricky bit for **you** is that what your child finds fun, new and attractive today may become taxing, old and boring tomorrow.

I: is for using an **Indirect** style when asking your child to comply with a demand. The more you depersonalise the request, the more likely your child is to feel less under pressure, such as 'Wouldn't it be nice if we share the drawing pencils?' Developing language scripts to be used at home, at school and anywhere else can really help, and these can be changed and updated. Practising using language that is less direct is a good idea. Here you have some examples to get you started: 'Going out to the park would be a fantastic plan for tomorrow' or 'It would be really great if someone would help me to tidy up the toys.'

N: is for **No sensory overload.** It is very important to be alert to detect when your child might be overstimulated, when there might be too much going on at the same time, and to be mindful of their sensory needs. Not doing so will probably contribute to pushing your child's anxiety to risky levels where you don't want them to be.

D: is for helping your child to **Develop good relationships** with you and with important others. No matter how strained the relationship with your child can be at times, it is essential to take time to nourish a positive and trusting relationship with him or her. A good starting point can be letting your child decide on an activity to do together, something that they will enjoy, on their terms. Sharing activities that your child enjoys can build bonds and help create opportunities for communication. It is also important to help your child develop collaborative relationships with their teachers and other professionals involved in their care and to offer lots of support to help them to navigate the often turbulent waters of friendships with their peer group. It is a must to share your understanding and approach to your child's difficulties with members of your family and trusted friends – who at times can play key roles in your support group – and, in the case of siblings, to provide them with age-appropriate information. The more insight and knowledge you pass on to them, the easier it will be for them to build up and maintain a good relationship with your child.

A: is for keeping in mind your child's **Anxiety**. Any effort to cut down their anxiety is incredibly worthwhile. Remember that their determination to avoid demands and to control their environment, you included, is **anxiety-driven**. A mother who had a daughter with PDA we worked with often used the expression of having developed over the years a 'radar' to detect changes in her daughter's anxiety levels, so when they were going up she would ease demands and try calming strategies and when going down and staying low, she knew she had a window of opportunity to give a more demanding task a go (such as having a look at this book!). These calmer times are good times to help your child to improve their tolerance to the distress triggered by demands and to sensitively attempt a gradual exposure to increasing demands. We cannot stress enough how important – though not an easy and quick task – it is to be in tune with your child's anxiety by learning how to read the signs of when it is going up or down.

P: is for **Prioritising**. When your child is distressed, it is very important to set up carefully which is your top priority, or which are the few priorities you want your child to follow; what is really essential for you and what is best to give a miss. Pick your battles!

I: is for having an **Individualised plan** that meets your child's needs at home, at school and everywhere. The approach to manage your child needs to be tailor-made to their specific needs and consistently shared with everyone involved in their care.

N: is for **No rushing the communication with your child**. Make sure you are giving your child plenty of time to process the question or information they are given, and for them to come up with an answer or an action without feeling under pressure to do so. If your child is feeling on edge, the time you need to allow for them to reply will have to be longer. We have experienced in our practice how rewarding *seriously* slowing down a conversation with a young person with PDA can be: some of the best reflections we got from them were obtained in this way.

Finally, a last word of advice before saying our goodbyes: **Please look after yourself!** Use whatever works for you to stay as calm and positive as humanly possible. We have witnessed the exhaustion and strain that parenting can cause and searching for the right resources for your child can also take a toll. You are certainly not alone in this! There is research showing this is true: the anxiety levels of parents of children who have PDA patterns of behaviour are higher than those of parents of children with autism and conduct disorder. Being calm and positive when you are being challenged by your child's daily avoidance of demands or when dealing with a meltdown is indeed not an easy task. We have seen that reminding yourself that your child's denial to do things is anxiety-driven and getting as many people as possible to support you in caring for your child – family members, trusted friends, professionals, parents' PDA support groups – are very valuable ways to help you in your parenting.

All good wishes,

Glòria and *Tamar*

The PDA glasses: An exercise for parents, teachers and all people caring for a child with PDA

In our experience these children and young people with PDA are the most fragile and vulnerable ones within the autism spectrum. We firmly believe that no effort should be spared to help them find their way in a world that makes them unimaginably anxious as they feel bombarded by the unspoken demands of society and the specific demands placed by others on them as well as by themselves. **Looking through PDA lenses, the world, with its never-ending demands, is perceived, especially when the child is in a high state of anxiety, as incredibly overwhelming, stressful, uncertain, confusing, exhausting, upsetting, scary and unpredictable (we could use so many more adjectives!).**

We have been told on many occasions by those caring for a child with PDA that the strategies used with children with more typical autism often don't work, leaving them powerless and frustrated. We invite those working with these children and young people to do a simple exercise: to put on these imaginary PDA glasses not only to work out and test strategies you want to use with them but also to understand what it is like being them.

We ourselves regularly do this exercise and had our glasses on while writing the text of the book and drawing the illustrations. In our experience, this exercise has not just fuelled our empathy for these children but also our commitment to try our best for them. Just spare a few minutes to put these PDA glasses on and then imagine how hard your commute to work or doing your shopping in the supermarket becomes. Putting on your PDA glasses when you are at your lowest and most exasperated point in your parenting can renew your energy and give you some much-needed patience.

We cannot stress enough how important it is that everyone involved in the care of a child with PDA accepts that **they do *not* have the natural ability to respond to demands**. The child is not being deliberately and intentionally provoking and manipulating. It is essential to remember this when you are about to lose your nerve in the face of your child's firm determination not to do what you really want them to do or when dealing with meltdowns. A mother, with whom Dr Glòria worked closely to help her with her child with PDA, had a younger child who suffered from diabetes. She once made a spot-on reflection: she recognised that it took her a long time to finally accept that her older child's brain was inherently wired *not* to comply with requests but compelled to avoid them at all costs due to feeling overwhelmingly anxious; conversely, it had been easy for her to get to grips with the fact that her younger child's pancreas was not able to produce insulin properly.

It is also useful to rephrase your internal dialogue to 'my child's anxiety is so through-the-roof that it is not letting them do what they are being asked to do'. This reinterpretation of your child's behaviour will not only help you to shape your reactions to their behaviour but also the way you feel about it.

Glòria Durà-Vilà

Dr Glòria Durà-Vilà, MD, MRCPsych, MSc, PhD, is a consultant child and adolescent psychiatrist and the medical lead for Autism Spectrum Disorder (ASD) in the Surrey and Borders Partnership NHS Foundation Trust. She has a main clinical interest in the assessment of ASD and the treatment of co-morbid mental health problems. She received a Clinical Excellence Award in 2018. She wrote the bestselling *My Autism Book: A Child's Guide to Their Autism Spectrum Diagnosis*, also published by Jessica Kingsley Publishers.

She is honorary lecturer at University College London, Division of Psychiatry and at Queen Mary University of London, Centre for Psychiatry, and was previously clinical lecturer at Imperial College London. Her research interests in the field of cultural psychiatry and medical anthropology include culture, spirituality and mental health, the medicalisation of sadness, and idioms of distress. Her book *Sadness, Depression and the Dark Night of the Soul: Transcending the Medicalisation of Sadness* was published in 2017 by Jessica Kingsley Publishers. She is a member of the executive committee of the Special Interest Groups of the Royal College of Psychiatrists for Spirituality and Psychiatry, and Transcultural Psychiatry.

Besides her NHS responsibilities, she also works in private practice, offers consultation and training to schools, and is in demand to present her research in national and international conferences. She was born in Spain but London has been her home since 2003. For more information, please see her website gloriaduravila.weebly.com

Tamar Levi

Alaskan raised, Cornish-Jewish, Brussels-based author and illustrator Tamar Levi has spent her life writing, reading and painting.

Beginning with degrees in philosophy and psychology at London and Cambridge University, Tamar went on to win an award for her research and illustrate award-winning books. For the past few years she has devoted her time to writing and exhibiting her artwork in galleries around Europe. This is her ninth children's book.

© Bengi Lostar Özdemir